BREEDER

Log Book Litters journal

PERSONAL INFORMATION

Name : _____

Address : _____

_____

_____

Email : _____

Phone : _____

Fax : _____

LOG BOOK INFORMATION

LOG BOOK START DATE	
LOG BOOK END DATE	
LOG BOOK NUMBER	

D1528082

We hope that this Book will be useful and, practical as we wanted to be.

If you think that this Book is good enough, and if it had been useful in any way, please make sure to LEAVE A REVIEW ON AMAZON REVIEW SECTION.

We would definitely love to read your honest opinions, and feedback, it will make us create better products for you in the future

THANK YOU VERY MUCH FOR YOU SUPPORT.

ANIMAL PROFILE RECORD BOOK

Name : ....

Date Of Birth : ....

Breed : ....

Tag #: ....

Registartion: ....

Sire Name : .... Sire # ....

Dam Name : .... Dam # ....

DATE	INCIDENT	NOTES

DATE	ITEM	COST

ANIMAL PROFILE RECORD BOOK

Name : ....

Date Of Birth : ....

Breed : ....

Tag #: ....

Registartion: ....

Sire Name : .... Sire # ....

Dam Name : .... Dam # ....

DATE	INCIDENT	NOTES

DATE	ITEM	COST

ANIMAL PROFILE RECORD BOOK

Name : ....

Date Of Birth : ....

Breed : ....

Tag #: ....

Registartion: ....

Sire Name : .... Sire # ....

Dam Name : .... Dam # ....

DATE	INCIDENT	NOTES

DATE	ITEM	COST

ANIMAL PROFILE RECORD BOOK

Name : ....

Date Of Birth : ....

Breed : ....

Tag #: ....

Registartion: ....

Sire Name : ....Sire # ....

Dam Name : .... Dam # ....

DATE	INCIDENT	NOTES

DATE	ITEM	COST

ANIMAL PROFILE RECORD BOOK

Name : ....
Date Of Birth : ....
Breed : ....
Tag #: ....
Registartion: ....
Sire Name : .... Sire # ....
Dam Name : .... Dam # ....

DATE	INCIDENT	NOTES

DATE	ITEM	COST

ANIMAL PROFILE RECORD BOOK

Name : ....

Date Of Birth : ....

Breed : ....

Tag #: ....

Registartion: ....

Sire Name : .... Sire # ....

Dam Name : .... Dam # ....

DATE	INCIDENT	NOTES

DATE	ITEM	COST

ANIMAL PROFILE RECORD BOOK

Name : ....

Date Of Birth : ....

Breed : ....

Tag #:...

Registartion: ....

Sire Name : .... Sire # ....

Dam Name : .... Dam # ....

DATE	INCIDENT	NOTES

DATE	ITEM	COST

ANIMAL PROFILE RECORD BOOK

Name : ....

Date Of Birth : ....

Breed : ....

Tag #:...

Registartion: ....

Sire Name : ....Sire # ....

Dam Name : .... Dam # ....

DATE	INCIDENT	NOTES

DATE	ITEM	COST

ANIMAL PROFILE RECORD BOOK

Name : ....

Date Of Birth : ....

Breed : ....

Tag #: ....

Registartion: ....

Sire Name : .... Sire # ....

Dam Name : .... Dam # ....

DATE	INCIDENT	NOTES

DATE	ITEM	COST

ANIMAL PROFILE RECORD BOOK

Name : ....

Date Of Birth : ....

Breed : ....

Tag #: ....

Registartion: ....

Sire Name : ....Sire # ....

Dam Name : .... Dam # ....

DATE	INCIDENT	NOTES

DATE	ITEM	COST

ANIMAL PROFILE RECORD BOOK

Name : ....
Date Of Birth : ....
Breed : ....
Tag #: ....
Registartion: ....
Sire Name : .... Sire # ....
Dam Name : .... Dam # ....

DATE	INCIDENT	NOTES

DATE	ITEM	COST

ANIMAL PROFILE RECORD BOOK

Name : ....

Date Of Birth : ....

Breed : ....

Tag #: ....

Registartion: ....

Sire Name : .... Sire # ....

Dam Name : .... Dam # ....

DATE	INCIDENT	NOTES

DATE	ITEM	COST

ANIMAL PROFILE RECORD BOOK

Name : ....

Date Of Birth : ....

Breed : ....

Tag #: ....

Registartion: ....

Sire Name : .... Sire # ....

Dam Name : .... Dam # ....

DATE	INCIDENT	NOTES

DATE	ITEM	COST

ANIMAL PROFILE RECORD BOOK

Name : ....

Date Of Birth : ....

Breed : ....

Tag #: ....

Registartion: ....

Sire Name : .... Sire # ....

Dam Name : .... Dam # ....

DATE	INCIDENT	NOTES

DATE	ITEM	COST

ANIMAL PROFILE RECORD BOOK

Name : ....

Date Of Birth : ....

Breed : ....

Tag #: ....

Registartion: ....

Sire Name : .... Sire # ....

Dam Name : .... Dam # ....

DATE	INCIDENT	NOTES

DATE	ITEM	COST

ANIMAL PROFILE RECORD BOOK

Name : ....

Date Of Birth : ....

Breed : ....

Tag #: ....

Registartion: ....

Sire Name : ....Sire # ....

Dam Name : .... Dam # ....

DATE	INCIDENT	NOTES

DATE	ITEM	COST

ANIMAL PROFILE RECORD BOOK

Name : ....

Date Of Birth : ....

Breed : ....

Tag #: ....

Registartion: ....

Sire Name : .... Sire # ....

Dam Name : .... Dam # ....

DATE	INCIDENT	NOTES

DATE	ITEM	COST

ANIMAL PROFILE RECORD BOOK

Name : ....

Date Of Birth : ....

Breed : ....

Tag #: ....

Registartion: ....

Sire Name : .... Sire # ....

Dam Name : .... Dam # ....

DATE	INCIDENT	NOTES

DATE	ITEM	COST

ANIMAL PROFILE RECORD BOOK

Name : ....

Date Of Birth : ....

Breed : ....

Tag #: ....

Registartion: ....

Sire Name : .... Sire # ....

Dam Name : .... Dam # ....

DATE	INCIDENT	NOTES

DATE	ITEM	COST

ANIMAL PROFILE RECORD BOOK

Name : ....

Date Of Birth : ....

Breed : ....

Tag #:...

Registartion: ....

Sire Name : .... Sire # ....

Dam Name : .... Dam # ....

DATE	INCIDENT	NOTES

DATE	ITEM	COST

ANIMAL PROFILE RECORD BOOK

Name : ....

Date Of Birth : ....

Breed : ....

Tag #: ....

Registartion: ....

Sire Name : .... Sire # ....

Dam Name : .... Dam # ....

DATE	INCIDENT	NOTES

DATE	ITEM	COST

ANIMAL PROFILE RECORD BOOK

Name : ....

Date Of Birth : ....

Breed : ....

Tag #: ....

Registartion: ....

Sire Name : ....Sire # ....

Dam Name : ....Dam # ....

DATE	INCIDENT	NOTES

DATE	ITEM	COST

ANIMAL PROFILE RECORD BOOK

Name : ....

Date Of Birth : ....

Breed : ....

Tag #: ....

Registartion: ....

Sire Name : .... Sire # ....

Dam Name : .... Dam # ....

DATE	INCIDENT	NOTES

DATE	ITEM	COST

ANIMAL PROFILE RECORD BOOK

Name : ....

Date Of Birth : ....

Breed : ....

Tag #: ....

Registartion: ....

Sire Name : .... Sire # ....

Dam Name : .... Dam # ....

DATE	INCIDENT	NOTES

DATE	ITEM	COST

ANIMAL PROFILE RECORD BOOK

Name : ....

Date Of Birth : ....

Breed : ....

Tag #: ....

Registartion: ....

Sire Name : .... Sire # ....

Dam Name : .... Dam # ....

DATE	INCIDENT	NOTES

DATE	ITEM	COST

ANIMAL PROFILE RECORD BOOK

Name : ....

Date Of Birth : ....

Breed : ....

Tag #: ....

Registartion: ....

Sire Name : .... Sire # ....

Dam Name : .... Dam # ....

DATE	INCIDENT	NOTES

DATE	ITEM	COST

ANIMAL PROFILE RECORD BOOK

Name : ....
Date Of Birth : ....
Breed : ....
Tag #: ....
Registartion: ....
Sire Name : .... Sire # ....
Dam Name : .... Dam # ....

DATE	INCIDENT	NOTES

DATE	ITEM	COST

ANIMAL PROFILE RECORD BOOK

Name : ....

Date Of Birth : ....

Breed : ....

Tag #: ....

Registartion: ....

Sire Name : ....Sire # ....

Dam Name : .... Dam # ....

DATE	INCIDENT	NOTES

DATE	ITEM	COST

ANIMAL PROFILE RECORD BOOK

Name : ....

Date Of Birth : ....

Breed : ....

Tag #: ....

Registartion: ....

Sire Name : .... Sire # ....

Dam Name : .... Dam # ....

DATE	INCIDENT	NOTES

DATE	ITEM	COST

ANIMAL PROFILE RECORD BOOK

Name : ....

Date Of Birth : ....

Breed : ....

Tag #: ....

Registartion: ....

Sire Name : .... Sire # ....

Dam Name : .... Dam # ....

DATE	INCIDENT	NOTES

DATE	ITEM	COST

ANIMAL PROFILE RECORD BOOK

Name : ....

Date Of Birth : ....

Breed : ....

Tag #: ....

Registartion: ....

Sire Name : .... Sire # ....

Dam Name : .... Dam # ....

DATE	INCIDENT	NOTES

DATE	ITEM	COST

ANIMAL PROFILE RECORD BOOK

Name : ....

Date Of Birth : ....

Breed : ....

Tag #: ....

Registartion: ....

Sire Name : .... Sire # ....

Dam Name : .... Dam # ....

DATE	INCIDENT	NOTES

DATE	ITEM	COST

ANIMAL PROFILE RECORD BOOK

Name : ....

Date Of Birth : ....

Breed : ....

Tag #: ....

Registartion: ....

Sire Name : ....Sire # ....

Dam Name : .... Dam # ....

DATE	INCIDENT	NOTES

DATE	ITEM	COST

ANIMAL PROFILE RECORD BOOK

Name : ....

Date Of Birth : ....

Breed : ....

Tag #: ....

Registartion: ....

Sire Name : ....Sire # ....

Dam Name : .... Dam # ....

DATE	INCIDENT	NOTES

DATE	ITEM	COST

ANIMAL PROFILE RECORD BOOK

Name : ....

Date Of Birth : ....

Breed : ....

Tag #: ....

Registartion: ....

Sire Name : .... Sire # ....

Dam Name : .... Dam # ....

DATE	INCIDENT	NOTES

DATE	ITEM	COST

ANIMAL PROFILE RECORD BOOK

Name : ....

Date Of Birth : ....

Breed : ....

Tag #: ....

Registartion: ....

Sire Name : .... Sire # ....

Dam Name : .... Dam # ....

DATE	INCIDENT	NOTES

DATE	ITEM	COST

ANIMAL PROFILE RECORD BOOK

Name : ....

Date Of Birth : ....

Breed : ....

Tag #: ....

Registartion: ....

Sire Name : .... Sire # ....

Dam Name : .... Dam # ....

DATE	INCIDENT	NOTES

DATE	ITEM	COST

ANIMAL PROFILE RECORD BOOK

Name : ....

Date Of Birth : ....

Breed : ....

Tag #: ....

Registartion: ....

Sire Name : .... Sire # ....

Dam Name : .... Dam # ....

DATE	INCIDENT	NOTES

DATE	ITEM	COST

ANIMAL PROFILE RECORD BOOK

Name : ....

Date Of Birth : ....

Breed : ....

Tag #: ....

Registartion: ....

Sire Name : .... Sire # ....

Dam Name : .... Dam # ....

DATE	INCIDENT	NOTES

DATE	ITEM	COST

ANIMAL PROFILE RECORD BOOK

Name : ....

Date Of Birth : ....

Breed : ....

Tag #: ....

Registartion: ....

Sire Name : ....Sire # ....

Dam Name : .... Dam # ....

DATE	INCIDENT	NOTES

DATE	ITEM	COST

ANIMAL PROFILE RECORD BOOK

Name : ....

Date Of Birth : ....

Breed : ....

Tag #: ....

Registartion: ....

Sire Name : .... Sire # ....

Dam Name : .... Dam # ....

DATE	INCIDENT	NOTES

DATE	ITEM	COST

ANIMAL PROFILE RECORD BOOK

Name : ....

Date Of Birth : ....

Breed : ....

Tag #: ....

Registartion: ....

Sire Name : ....Sire # ....

Dam Name : .... Dam # ....

DATE	INCIDENT	NOTES

DATE	ITEM	COST

ANIMAL PROFILE RECORD BOOK

Name : ....

Date Of Birth : ....

Breed : ....

Tag #: ....

Registartion: ....

Sire Name : .... Sire # ....

Dam Name : .... Dam # ....

DATE	INCIDENT	NOTES

DATE	ITEM	COST

ANIMAL PROFILE RECORD BOOK

Name : ....
Date Of Birth : ....
Breed : ....
Tag #: ....
Registartion: ....
Sire Name : ....Sire # ....
Dam Name : .... Dam # ....

DATE	INCIDENT	NOTES

DATE	ITEM	COST

ANIMAL PROFILE RECORD BOOK

Name : ....

Date Of Birth : ....

Breed : ....

Tag #: ....

Registartion: ....

Sire Name : ....Sire # ....

Dam Name : ....Dam # ....

DATE	INCIDENT	NOTES

DATE	ITEM	COST

ANIMAL PROFILE RECORD BOOK

Name : ....

Date Of Birth : ....

Breed : ....

Tag #: ....

Registartion: ....

Sire Name : .... Sire # ....

Dam Name : .... Dam # ....

DATE	INCIDENT	NOTES

DATE	ITEM	COST

ANIMAL PROFILE RECORD BOOK

Name : ....

Date Of Birth : ....

Breed : ....

Tag #: ....

Registartion: ....

Sire Name : .... Sire # ....

Dam Name : .... Dam # ....

DATE	INCIDENT	NOTES

DATE	ITEM	COST

ANIMAL PROFILE RECORD BOOK

Name : ....

Date Of Birth : ....

Breed : ....

Tag #: ....

Registartion: ....

Sire Name : .... Sire # ....

Dam Name : .... Dam # ....

DATE	INCIDENT	NOTES

DATE	ITEM	COST

ANIMAL PROFILE RECORD BOOK

Name : ....

Date Of Birth : ....

Breed : ....

Tag #: ....

Registartion: ....

Sire Name : .... Sire # ....

Dam Name : .... Dam # ....

DATE	INCIDENT	NOTES

DATE	ITEM	COST

ANIMAL PROFILE RECORD BOOK

Name : ....

Date Of Birth : ....

Breed : ....

Tag #: ....

Registartion: ....

Sire Name : .... Sire # ....

Dam Name : .... Dam # ....

DATE	INCIDENT	NOTES

DATE	ITEM	COST

ANIMAL PROFILE RECORD BOOK

Name : ....
Date Of Birth : ....
Breed : ....
Tag #: ....
Registartion: ....
Sire Name : .... Sire # ....
Dam Name : .... Dam # ....

DATE	INCIDENT	NOTES

DATE	ITEM	COST

ANIMAL PROFILE RECORD BOOK

Name : ....

Date Of Birth : ....

Breed : ....

Tag #: ....

Registartion: ....

Sire Name : ....Sire # ....

Dam Name : .... Dam # ....

DATE	INCIDENT	NOTES

DATE	ITEM	COST

ANIMAL PROFILE RECORD BOOK

Name : ....

Date Of Birth : ....

Breed : ....

Tag #: ....

Registartion: ....

Sire Name : .... Sire # ....

Dam Name : .... Dam # ....

DATE	INCIDENT	NOTES

DATE	ITEM	COST

ANIMAL PROFILE RECORD BOOK

Name : ....

Date Of Birth : ....

Breed : ....

Tag #: ....

Registartion: ....

Sire Name : .... Sire # ....

Dam Name : .... Dam # ....

DATE	INCIDENT	NOTES

DATE	ITEM	COST

ANIMAL PROFILE RECORD BOOK

Name : ....

Date Of Birth : ....

Breed : ....

Tag #: ....

Registartion: ....

Sire Name : .... Sire # ....

Dam Name : .... Dam # ....

DATE	INCIDENT	NOTES

DATE	ITEM	COST

ANIMAL PROFILE RECORD BOOK

Name : ....

Date Of Birth : ....

Breed : ....

Tag #: ....

Registartion: ....

Sire Name : .... Sire # ....

Dam Name : .... Dam # ....

DATE	INCIDENT	NOTES

DATE	ITEM	COST

ANIMAL PROFILE RECORD BOOK

Name : ....

Date Of Birth : ....

Breed : ....

Tag #: ....

Registartion: ....

Sire Name : .... Sire # ....

Dam Name : .... Dam # ....

DATE	INCIDENT	NOTES

DATE	ITEM	COST

ANIMAL PROFILE RECORD BOOK

Name : ....

Date Of Birth : ....

Breed : ....

Tag #: ....

Registartion: ....

Sire Name : .... Sire # ....

Dam Name : .... Dam # ....

DATE	INCIDENT	NOTES

DATE	ITEM	COST

ANIMAL PROFILE RECORD BOOK

Name : ....
Date Of Birth : ....
Breed : ....
Tag #: ....
Registartion: ....
Sire Name : .... Sire # ....
Dam Name : .... Dam # ....

DATE	INCIDENT	NOTES

DATE	ITEM	COST

ANIMAL PROFILE RECORD BOOK

Name : ....

Date Of Birth : ....

Breed : ....

Tag #: ....

Registartion: ....

Sire Name : .... Sire # ....

Dam Name : .... Dam # ....

DATE	INCIDENT	NOTES

DATE	ITEM	COST

ANIMAL PROFILE RECORD BOOK

Name : ....

Date Of Birth : ....

Breed : ....

Tag #: ....

Registartion: ....

Sire Name : .... Sire # ....

Dam Name : .... Dam # ....

DATE	INCIDENT	NOTES

DATE	ITEM	COST

ANIMAL PROFILE RECORD BOOK

Name : ....

Date Of Birth : ....

Breed : ....

Tag #: ....

Registartion: ....

Sire Name : .... Sire # ....

Dam Name : .... Dam # ....

DATE	INCIDENT	NOTES

DATE	ITEM	COST

ANIMAL PROFILE RECORD BOOK

Name : ....

Date Of Birth : ....

Breed : ....

Tag #: ....

Registartion: ....

Sire Name : .... Sire # ....

Dam Name : .... Dam # ....

DATE	INCIDENT	NOTES

DATE	ITEM	COST

ANIMAL PROFILE RECORD BOOK

Name : ....

Date Of Birth : ....

Breed : ....

Tag #: ....

Registartion: ....

Sire Name : ....Sire # ....

Dam Name : .... Dam # ....

DATE	INCIDENT	NOTES

DATE	ITEM	COST

ANIMAL PROFILE RECORD BOOK

Name : ....
Date Of Birth : ....
Breed : ....
Tag #: ....
Registartion: ....
Sire Name : .... Sire # ....
Dam Name : .... Dam # ....

DATE	INCIDENT	NOTES

DATE	ITEM	COST

ANIMAL PROFILE RECORD BOOK

Name : ....

Date Of Birth : ....

Breed : ....

Tag #: ....

Registartion: ....

Sire Name : .... Sire # ....

Dam Name : .... Dam # ....

DATE	INCIDENT	NOTES

DATE	ITEM	COST

ANIMAL PROFILE RECORD BOOK

Name : ....

Date Of Birth : ....

Breed : ....

Tag #: ....

Registartion: ....

Sire Name : .... Sire # ....

Dam Name : .... Dam # ....

DATE	INCIDENT	NOTES

DATE	ITEM	COST

ANIMAL PROFILE RECORD BOOK

Name : ....

Date Of Birth : ....

Breed : ....

Tag #: ....

Registartion: ....

Sire Name : .... Sire # ....

Dam Name : .... Dam # ....

DATE	INCIDENT	NOTES

DATE	ITEM	COST

ANIMAL PROFILE RECORD BOOK

Name : ....

Date Of Birth : ....

Breed : ....

Tag #: ....

Registartion: ....

Sire Name : .... Sire # ....

Dam Name : .... Dam # ....

DATE	INCIDENT	NOTES

DATE	ITEM	COST

ANIMAL PROFILE RECORD BOOK

Name : ....

Date Of Birth : ....

Breed : ....

Tag #: ....

Registartion: ....

Sire Name : ....Sire # ....

Dam Name : .... Dam # ....

DATE	INCIDENT	NOTES

DATE	ITEM	COST

ANIMAL PROFILE RECORD BOOK

Name : ....
Date Of Birth : ....
Breed : ....
Tag #: ....
Registartion: ....
Sire Name : .... Sire # ....
Dam Name : .... Dam # ....

DATE	INCIDENT	NOTES

DATE	ITEM	COST

ANIMAL PROFILE RECORD BOOK

Name : ....

Date Of Birth : ....

Breed : ....

Tag #: ....

Registartion: ....

Sire Name : .... Sire # ....

Dam Name : .... Dam # ....

DATE	INCIDENT	NOTES

DATE	ITEM	COST

ANIMAL PROFILE RECORD BOOK

Name : ....

Date Of Birth : ....

Breed : ....

Tag #: ....

Registartion: ....

Sire Name : .... Sire # ....

Dam Name : .... Dam # ....

DATE	INCIDENT	NOTES

DATE	ITEM	COST

ANIMAL PROFILE RECORD BOOK

Name : ....

Date Of Birth : ....

Breed : ....

Tag #: ....

Registartion: ....

Sire Name : .... Sire # ....

Dam Name : .... Dam # ....

DATE	INCIDENT	NOTES

DATE	ITEM	COST

ANIMAL PROFILE RECORD BOOK

Name : ....

Date Of Birth : ....

Breed : ....

Tag #: ....

Registartion: ....

Sire Name : .... Sire # ....

Dam Name : .... Dam # ....

DATE	INCIDENT	NOTES

DATE	ITEM	COST

ANIMAL PROFILE RECORD BOOK

Name : ....

Date Of Birth : ....

Breed : ....

Tag #: ....

Registartion: ....

Sire Name : .... Sire # ....

Dam Name : .... Dam # ....

DATE	INCIDENT	NOTES

DATE	ITEM	COST

ANIMAL PROFILE RECORD BOOK

Name : ....
Date Of Birth : ....
Breed : ....
Tag #: ....
Registartion: ....
Sire Name : .... Sire # ....
Dam Name : .... Dam # ....

DATE	INCIDENT	NOTES

DATE	ITEM	COST

ANIMAL PROFILE RECORD BOOK

Name : ....

Date Of Birth : ....

Breed : ....

Tag #: ....

Registartion: ....

Sire Name : .... Sire # ....

Dam Name : .... Dam # ....

DATE	INCIDENT	NOTES

DATE	ITEM	COST

ANIMAL PROFILE RECORD BOOK

Name : ....

Date Of Birth : ....

Breed : ....

Tag #:...

Registartion: ....

Sire Name : .... Sire # ....

Dam Name : .... Dam # ....

DATE	INCIDENT	NOTES

DATE	ITEM	COST

ANIMAL PROFILE RECORD BOOK

Name : ....

Date Of Birth : ....

Breed : ....

Tag #: ....

Registartion: ....

Sire Name : .... Sire # ....

Dam Name : .... Dam # ....

DATE	INCIDENT	NOTES

DATE	ITEM	COST

ANIMAL PROFILE RECORD BOOK

Name : ....

Date Of Birth : ....

Breed : ....

Tag #: ....

Registartion: ....

Sire Name : .... Sire # ....

Dam Name : .... Dam # ....

DATE	INCIDENT	NOTES

DATE	ITEM	COST

ANIMAL PROFILE RECORD BOOK

Name : ....

Date Of Birth : ....

Breed : ....

Tag #: ....

Registartion: ....

Sire Name : ....Sire # ....

Dam Name : .... Dam # ....

DATE	INCIDENT	NOTES

DATE	ITEM	COST

ANIMAL PROFILE RECORD BOOK

Name : ....

Date Of Birth : ....

Breed : ....

Tag #: ....

Registartion: ....

Sire Name : .... Sire # ....

Dam Name : .... Dam # ....

DATE	INCIDENT	NOTES

DATE	ITEM	COST

ANIMAL PROFILE RECORD BOOK

Name : ....

Date Of Birth : ....

Breed : ....

Tag #: ....

Registartion: ....

Sire Name : .... Sire # ....

Dam Name : .... Dam # ....

DATE	INCIDENT	NOTES

DATE	ITEM	COST

ANIMAL PROFILE RECORD BOOK

Name : ....

Date Of Birth : ....

Breed : ....

Tag #: ....

Registartion: ....

Sire Name : .... Sire # ....

Dam Name : .... Dam # ....

DATE	INCIDENT	NOTES

DATE	ITEM	COST

ANIMAL PROFILE RECORD BOOK

Name : ....

Date Of Birth : ....

Breed : ....

Tag #: ....

Registartion: ....

Sire Name : .... Sire # ....

Dam Name : .... Dam # ....

DATE	INCIDENT	NOTES

DATE	ITEM	COST

ANIMAL PROFILE RECORD BOOK

Name : ....

Date Of Birth : ....

Breed : ....

Tag #: ....

Registartion: ....

Sire Name : ....Sire # ....

Dam Name : ....Dam # ....

DATE	INCIDENT	NOTES

DATE	ITEM	COST

ANIMAL PROFILE RECORD BOOK

Name : ....

Date Of Birth : ....

Breed : ....

Tag #: ....

Registartion: ....

Sire Name : ....Sire # ....

Dam Name : .... Dam # ....

DATE	INCIDENT	NOTES

DATE	ITEM	COST

ANIMAL PROFILE RECORD BOOK

Name : ....

Date Of Birth : ....

Breed : ....

Tag #: ....

Registartion: ....

Sire Name : .... Sire # ....

Dam Name : .... Dam # ....

DATE	INCIDENT	NOTES

DATE	ITEM	COST

ANIMAL PROFILE RECORD BOOK

Name : ....

Date Of Birth : ....

Breed : ....

Tag #: ....

Registartion: ....

Sire Name : ....Sire # ....

Dam Name : .... Dam # ....

DATE	INCIDENT	NOTES

DATE	ITEM	COST

ANIMAL PROFILE RECORD BOOK

Name : ....

Date Of Birth : ....

Breed : ....

Tag #: ....

Registartion: ....

Sire Name : .... Sire # ....

Dam Name : .... Dam # ....

DATE	INCIDENT	NOTES

DATE	ITEM	COST

ANIMAL PROFILE RECORD BOOK

Name : ....
Date Of Birth : ....
Breed : ....
Tag #: ....
Registartion: ....
Sire Name : .... Sire # ....
Dam Name : .... Dam # ....

DATE	INCIDENT	NOTES

DATE	ITEM	COST

ANIMAL PROFILE RECORD BOOK

Name : ....

Date Of Birth : ....

Breed : ....

Tag #: ....

Registartion: ....

Sire Name : .... Sire # ....

Dam Name : .... Dam # ....

DATE	INCIDENT	NOTES

DATE	ITEM	COST

ANIMAL PROFILE RECORD BOOK

Name : ....

Date Of Birth : ....

Breed : ....

Tag #: ....

Registartion: ....

Sire Name : .... Sire # ....

Dam Name : .... Dam # ....

DATE	INCIDENT	NOTES

DATE	ITEM	COST

ANIMAL PROFILE RECORD BOOK

Name : ....

Date Of Birth : ....

Breed : ....

Tag #: ....

Registartion: ....

Sire Name : .... Sire # ....

Dam Name : .... Dam # ....

DATE	INCIDENT	NOTES

DATE	ITEM	COST

ANIMAL PROFILE RECORD BOOK

Name : ....

Date Of Birth : ....

Breed : ....

Tag #: ....

Registartion: ....

Sire Name : ....Sire # ....

Dam Name : .... Dam # ....

DATE	INCIDENT	NOTES

DATE	ITEM	COST

ANIMAL PROFILE RECORD BOOK

Name : ....

Date Of Birth : ....

Breed : ....

Tag #: ....

Registartion: ....

Sire Name : .... Sire # ....

Dam Name : .... Dam # ....

DATE	INCIDENT	NOTES

DATE	ITEM	COST

ANIMAL PROFILE RECORD BOOK

Name : ....

Date Of Birth : ....

Breed : ....

Tag #: ....

Registartion: ....

Sire Name : ....Sire # ....

Dam Name : .... Dam # ....

DATE	INCIDENT	NOTES

DATE	ITEM	COST

ANIMAL PROFILE RECORD BOOK

Name : ....

Date Of Birth : ....

Breed : ....

Tag #: ....

Registartion: ....

Sire Name : .... Sire # ....

Dam Name : .... Dam # ....

DATE	INCIDENT	NOTES

DATE	ITEM	COST

ANIMAL PROFILE RECORD BOOK

Name : ....

Date Of Birth : ....

Breed : ....

Tag #: ....

Registartion: ....

Sire Name : .... Sire # ....

Dam Name : .... Dam # ....

DATE	INCIDENT	NOTES

DATE	ITEM	COST

ANIMAL PROFILE RECORD BOOK

Name : ....

Date Of Birth : ....

Breed : ....

Tag #: ....

Registartion: ....

Sire Name : .... Sire # ....

Dam Name : .... Dam # ....

DATE	INCIDENT	NOTES

DATE	ITEM	COST

ANIMAL PROFILE RECORD BOOK

Name : ....

Date Of Birth : ....

Breed : ....

Tag #: ....

Registartion: ....

Sire Name : .... Sire # ....

Dam Name : .... Dam # ....

DATE	INCIDENT	NOTES

DATE	ITEM	COST

ANIMAL PROFILE RECORD BOOK

Name : ....

Date Of Birth : ....

Breed : ....

Tag #: ....

Registartion: ....

Sire Name : ....Sire # ....

Dam Name : .... Dam # ....

DATE	INCIDENT	NOTES

DATE	ITEM	COST

ANIMAL PROFILE RECORD BOOK

Name : ....

Date Of Birth : ....

Breed : ....

Tag #: ....

Registartion: ....

Sire Name : .... Sire # ....

Dam Name : .... Dam # ....

DATE	INCIDENT	NOTES

DATE	ITEM	COST

ANIMAL PROFILE RECORD BOOK

Name : ....

Date Of Birth : ....

Breed : ....

Tag #: ....

Registartion: ....

Sire Name : .... Sire # ....

Dam Name : .... Dam # ....

DATE	INCIDENT	NOTES

DATE	ITEM	COST

ANIMAL PROFILE RECORD BOOK

Name : ....

Date Of Birth : ....

Breed : ....

Tag #: ....

Registartion: ....

Sire Name : .... Sire # ....

Dam Name : .... Dam # ....

DATE	INCIDENT	NOTES

DATE	ITEM	COST

ANIMAL PROFILE RECORD BOOK

Name : ....

Date Of Birth : ....

Breed : ....

Tag #: ....

Registartion: ....

Sire Name : .... Sire # ....

Dam Name : .... Dam # ....

DATE	INCIDENT	NOTES

DATE	ITEM	COST

ANIMAL PROFILE RECORD BOOK

Name : ....

Date Of Birth : ....

Breed : ....

Tag #: ....

Registartion: ....

Sire Name : .... Sire # ....

Dam Name : .... Dam # ....

DATE	INCIDENT	NOTES

DATE	ITEM	COST

ANIMAL PROFILE RECORD BOOK

Name : ....
Date Of Birth : ....
Breed : ....
Tag #: ....
Registartion: ....
Sire Name : ....Sire # ....
Dam Name : .... Dam # ....

DATE	INCIDENT	NOTES

DATE	ITEM	COST

ANIMAL PROFILE RECORD BOOK

Name : ....

Date Of Birth : ....

Breed : ....

Tag #: ....

Registartion: ....

Sire Name : .... Sire # ....

Dam Name : .... Dam # ....

DATE	INCIDENT	NOTES

DATE	ITEM	COST

ANIMAL PROFILE RECORD BOOK

Name : ....

Date Of Birth : ....

Breed : ....

Tag #: ....

Registartion: ....

Sire Name : .... Sire # ....

Dam Name : .... Dam # ....

DATE	INCIDENT	NOTES

DATE	ITEM	COST

ANIMAL PROFILE RECORD BOOK

Name : ....

Date Of Birth : ....

Breed : ....

Tag #: ....

Registartion: ....

Sire Name : .... Sire # ....

Dam Name : .... Dam # ....

DATE	INCIDENT	NOTES

DATE	ITEM	COST

ANIMAL PROFILE RECORD BOOK

Name : ....

Date Of Birth : ....

Breed : ....

Tag #: ....

Registartion: ....

Sire Name : .... Sire # ....

Dam Name : .... Dam # ....

DATE	INCIDENT	NOTES

DATE	ITEM	COST

ANIMAL PROFILE RECORD BOOK

Name : ....
Date Of Birth : ....
Breed : ....
Tag #: ....
Registartion: ....
Sire Name : .... Sire # ....
Dam Name : .... Dam # ....

DATE	INCIDENT	NOTES

DATE	ITEM	COST

ANIMAL PROFILE RECORD BOOK

Name : ....

Date Of Birth : ....

Breed : ....

Tag #: ....

Registartion: ....

Sire Name : .... Sire # ....

Dam Name : .... Dam # ....

DATE	INCIDENT	NOTES

DATE	ITEM	COST

ANIMAL PROFILE RECORD BOOK

Name : ....
Date Of Birth : ....
Breed : ....
Tag #: ....
Registartion: ....
Sire Name : .... Sire # ....
Dam Name : .... Dam # ....

DATE	INCIDENT	NOTES

DATE	ITEM	COST

ANIMAL PROFILE RECORD BOOK

Name : ....

Date Of Birth : ....

Breed : ....

Tag #: ....

Registartion: ....

Sire Name : .... Sire # ....

Dam Name : .... Dam # ....

DATE	INCIDENT	NOTES

DATE	ITEM	COST

ANIMAL PROFILE RECORD BOOK

Name : ....

Date Of Birth : ....

Breed : ....

Tag #: ....

Registartion: ....

Sire Name : .... Sire # ....

Dam Name : .... Dam # ....

DATE	INCIDENT	NOTES

DATE	ITEM	COST

Made in the USA
Monee, IL
18 March 2022

93088184R00069